A Commentary on the Possible Future of Society
(A Guide to Utopia)

Foreword

In the following pages I pursue some fairly startling ideas, or extensions of existing ideas, in a fairly concentrated (if somewhat haphazard) manner. I make no apology for this, as ideas are ideas and do not need a mass of verbiage or a particular sequence to justify them. Some may be naïve. They will either stand up under the eye of future knowledge, or they will not. In addition an abrupt approach tends to shock the reader, either into a dismissive reaction or a thoughtful one. I am certain that a lot of readers will have the first reaction. This short book is written for those who have the second.

Contents

A Commentary on the Possible Future of Society
(A Guide to Utopia)

Introduction

The time must be fast approaching when humanity will have to take a global view of itself and its environment, particularly with regard to population control and the encouragement of a better level of education, and hopefully to some degree intelligence, world-wide. Let me hasten to add that I am not thereby implying my own intelligence is any great shakes, I am perfectly well aware that it isn't, it's just that viewing the world as it is today I, or indeed anyone, can see such an appalling lack of common sense that I feel compelled to write something about it. We are fast approaching a knowledge of genetic engineering which will enable civilization to improve its genes, anathema as this might be to many, many people. It would be evolution by other means, and if it is not to result in two classes, or indeed types, of human being (those who can afford it and those who can't), will require a limiting of population, the advance of technology, an enlightened government and a great deal of common sense. This commodity is so sadly lacking in today's world that I fear it will require a world-wide catastrophe of some sort, leading to a sweeping away of current political, religious and social institutions, before it has a chance to develop.

Apart from humanitarian problems two main problems in today's world would appear to be religion and tribalism, the latter being an example of an animal instinct and therefore not the same as nationalism, although nationalism can also exert a strong influence of course. Often tribes or races and nations coincide, but in many part of the world they don't. Tribalism could perhaps be made less of a problem if tribal boundaries replaced national ones. Drawing straight lines to create national boundaries, as in the past, usually by the victors after a war, is in retrospect somewhat ridiculous, and has caused endless trouble.

The problem of the Islamic religion is more difficult, since inherent in it seems to be a certain lack of common sense. I suppose a Muslim might say something like that about Christianity, particularly Roman Catholicism, even though the roots of the religions are basically similar, as is Judaism. Imagine if cosmology could be made a compulsory subject in madrasahs, presenting an opposing view of existence compared to a belief in a God, would that help? Probably not, because even a cosmologist can still believe in God, if he or she wants to, and Islam tends to fanaticism, where argument is useless anyway.

Also I think society will come to realise that it must punish criminality in a way that will really deter others (Islam has got that right). If in the future population has to be limited, society will not want to waste precious resources on negative elements. Consider the following possible future scenario:-

"The World Council for Social Engineering (against strong opposition from human rights groups) has proposed the following:-

It is obvious that the greatest long-term threat to the human race, apart from natural disasters, is over-population. Any conventional measures eventually taken to limit the global population will probably be too late, and will also raise difficult questions

1

about the value and sanctity of a human life. In this proposal we wish to consider the reversal of the conventional view of the sanctity of human life, and of foetal life, which we think will be necessary. It will look like eugenics, the long discredited idea of genetic purity which led to the Nazi concept of racial purity. But that would be a superficial view. The point to consider is that it will become necessary for us to realise that human life proliferates and is not sacred. Also for a society where population is controlled, surely it follows that each life must be of value to that society, i.e. productive, otherwise why, with limited population and resources, should that society support it? We should therefore attempt to eradicate the probably obese, unintelligent, expensive, useless, socially negative or criminal population, the parasitic element in society, by radical but socially acceptable means, mainly by perhaps radical educational means, perhaps removing some children from their parents for a period, as in a kibbutz or boarding school, and instilling self-discipline, self-respect and respect for others, leading to a socially productive life.

The main motivation of most of humanity is self-interest, quite understandably. But a significant part of humanity practises self-interest at the expense of others. "For the triumph of evil, it is only necessary that good men do nothing". Let us therefore, as a starting point for discussion, take an extreme view, the establishment of a Right to Life. It would require a charter, such as follows:-

1. Every member of society, on being born, has the right to life.

2. A board of appropriately qualified members would consider the rescinding of that right in the case of serious anti-social behaviour, particularly where the person has been convicted of :-

   a. first degree murder
   b. rape
   c. paedophilia
   d. a history of violence
   e. a history of criminality

   The board would also consider the sterilization of persons with an hereditary genetic abnormality leading to mental or physical conditions which render those persons violent or incapable of being a productive member of society, whilst being a drain on the resources of that society. Such persons would have slipped through the foetal examination mentioned below. Persons becoming mentally unstable after being born, but with no genetic disorder, would be cared for by the state.

3. A second board of appropriately qualified members would consider the fate of all persons where the right to life has been rescinded. Considerations would be any concerns about the verdict, the risk of re-offending and the deterrence of others. Psychological factors affecting the degree of guilt, such as childhood abuse or perhaps defective genes, would be of lesser importance, and also difficult to establish and difficult to quantify. The harshest decision would be a painless death. The board would also consider the fate of actual or potential abnormal foetuses, whilst allowing for possible evolutionary genetic

mutations. The presumption would be the possibility of correction or avoidance by genetic engineering.

4. Persons with a degenerative or unbearable condition would have the right to end their own life.

5. Persons would have the right to be tested for defective genes, and as a result, if necessary, could choose to make use of genetic engineering in respect of future children. Gradually defective genes in the gene pool should thus be drastically reduced."

Such a proposal and such a charter would establish the good of society as having precedence over the rights of the individual. This of course is very dangerous – it is how a police state operates. So we must be mindful of the difference between justice and the law. Would it be possible for a democratic government to operate such a charter? I don't see why not, if the people so choose. After all, capital punishment is the case in several American states and other parts of the world today.

Other social problems, such as population control by the limitation of births, care of the elderly and the drug problem would obviously need solutions, preferably by putting them into the hands of the state, which in the case of drugs would mean their ready availability from the state, but with the possibility of proper control of the problem. Taking drugs and prostitution out of the hands of criminals and into the hands of the state makes a lot of common sense, particularly if one takes a common sense view of human nature. Criminals must be laughing all the way to the bank at the inability of society to deal with the baser instincts of human nature. Thankfully many governments have at least seen the sense in taking over some of the many forms of gambling, particularly as they are usually spectacular sources of income. Could people be allowed to opt out and live outside such a world society somewhere? Since no laws would apply, such a community would be anarchic.

Let us consider the ideal society a little further. Surely the ideal society would be one in which the members were of one tribe, so there would be no internal racial or inter-tribal factions, and the charter above would clearly be of great benefit to the future of the tribe.

Ideally the tribe would live within tribal boundaries, reducing tension with neighbours. And ideally it would take account of the fact that a human is an animal, with animal instincts – a viewpoint that, amongst other things, we explore in this book and that we studiously ignore to the detriment of our societies. Would it be possible to extend this fundamental view of humanity to a possible future global UN government of many tribal types? It would need to be a federated constitution, the move towards this being perhaps initiated by the powerful influence of huge international conglomerates. America has managed it and Europe is trying to, so far with dubious success, mainly due to tribal differences between North and South. Tribal differences are also why any unconsidered immigration can be so harmful.

Let me expand further in a rather more utopian way on the concept of an ideal society, although it involves some repetition of ideas mentioned above. We live on a planet of almost incredibly beautiful biodiversity, but mankind detracts from it. The rise in recent years of the science of cosmology, mainly in the West, has confirmed what Darwin started, that belief in a God is becoming almost an anachronism, although this is fiercely resisted. So I think mankind, at some fundamental instinctive level, is still searching for a raison d'etre, a reason for leading a "good" life, and hasn't found it yet, except in religion. Thus today, to put it simplistically, we have decadence in the West, brain-washed fundamentalism in the East and Middle East and corruption in Africa and South America. There are problems on all major land masses, although isolated "tribal" societies like island communities have far fewer problems. Wars are endemic. Corrupt politicians and world-wide criminal networks abound. Thankfully the time of early religious, land and political wars seems to be behind us. Now it's mainly one religious war and tribal wars. What could be more of a contradiction in terms than a modern religious war? Is that civilized? From all these problems it is clear that it's time mankind realised we are still at the dawn of civilization, and man's animal instincts still largely lead human society by the nose, thinly veiled by civilization. To progress on the road to a truly civilized society we need to realise that we must design such a society by basing it on those animal instincts, whilst preserving our habitat. Thus we should agree clear tribal boundaries using the UN and referendums, re-defining national boundaries if feasible. Also agree population controls and the use of genetic engineering. In medicine ensure the emphasis is on prevention rather than cure, an obvious step that we still don't seem to have mastered, for instance the problems of obesity and alcohol abuse in the West, which should become more socially unacceptable. Indeed treatment for those who fail to look after themselves should receive low priority. Possibly establish where necessary a type of kibbutz based education away from inadequate or undesirable parents, based on rewarding effort and instilling self-discipline, self-respect and respect for others, otherwise there may always be an underclass of criminals. Drastically outlaw anti-social behaviour and criminality in all its forms. Establish peer group challenges for young men (enlarged on later). Agree habitat preserving measures and live in harmony with the planet. And finally apply the criterion of the greatest good for the greatest number. Our philosophy should be that everything we do is for the benefit of the children of our species. There is no afterlife. There is no deep cosmic philosophy. Frighteningly we are just one tiny planet in an unimaginably huge universe. Our children are why we are here, that is the lesson of life and evolution.

The following two quotations are from newspaper articles published over a decade ago, the first of which I have included for balance, as it presents a somewhat opposing view to the idea of looking at society from an animalistic point of view, however it goes on to advocate hunter-gathering, a clearly animalistic type activity:, as opposed to agriculture, which is not:-

1. "By inventing a culture whereby the experience gained by individuals in one generation can be handed on to the next, we have, to some extent, escaped the constraints of Darwinian evolution. If you seek the source of the success of homo-sapiens, behold the schoolteacher.

Ours is a double life: our cultural inheritance sets us apart from animals, but we have a biological inheritance. For a couple of decades now there has been a busy little industry, called socio-biology, which attempts to seek parallels from the animal kingdom with our social and cultural lives.

Socio-biology is, in my view, a deeply suspect enterprise. It risks a double jeopardy. One problem is that by explaining some unpleasant aspects of human behaviour – aggression, rape, war – in terms of the allegedly similar actions performed by animals, there is a risk of excusing the behaviour. To describe aggression say as "natural", because animals living in a state of nature exhibit aggression, is not very far from expressing approval of it: as the supermarkets and the advertising men know very well, the word "natural" has become synonymous with "good". It is of little avail to claim that it has a specialised usage, which means "living in a state of nature", because the moral ambiguity is now inherent in the word.

There is a view that agriculture was a really bad idea and that we would all be better off as hunter-gatherers – far more leisure time, far less disease, and plenty to eat. The invention of agriculture promoted social division: in a hunter-gatherer society, everyone had to get out there to hunt and gather: only with settled farming could princes and kings live off the fat of the land, or more correctly, off the sweated labour of their peasants. And without agriculture we would have no socio-biology".

2. "Sir ------- said there were 5.3 billion people in the world today, and that would rise to 8 billion by 2025, perhaps even 14 billion after that. Even allowing for war, famine and disease, the rate of increase, perhaps – at present some 90 million more people every year – suggests we are on the back of a tiger.

If everyone in the world became vegetarian and shared food equally, the planet could comfortably support 6 billion people. But if 35% of our calories came from animal products, as in North America now, then the world would only be able to sustain 2.5 billion people.

Competition for fresh water and fishing were likely flashpoints for future conflict. The global use of water doubled between 1940 and 1980 and was likely to double again before 2000.

Sir ------- foresaw the emergence of new patterns of human disease, partly as a result of an increase in global temperature and humidity, which are critical for viruses, bacteria and insects to multiply. At the same time, scientists would be less able to develop new drugs to fight them, with the loss of exotic species of plants from the dwindling rainforests – a prime source of new medicines. The extinction of plant and animal species was a major threat.

The ecosystem could be likened to a boat. We can remove one, two or ten rivets without apparent damage. But at a certain point – it could be the eleventh or the thousandth rivet – we cause the timbers to fall apart".

Chapter 1

Basic Instincts

In the course of evolution many mammals have become gregarious, living in tribal groups or smaller social groupings within the tribe, a way of life which has evolved with the taxonomic group (mammals) as the best vehicle for the survival of much of that group. Smaller groupings often have a well-defined social structure. Man is one such mammal. However man is intelligent and self-aware. His knowledge accumulates as he passes it from one generation to the next. He has morals and even ethics which he hopes modify or channel his basic instincts such that they can be contained within a social structure. So we have an animal, driven by basic instincts, albeit channelled, and yet able to reason consciously to what seems to be a remarkable degree, in that he has achieved a degree of understanding of the universe around him. What a remarkable anomaly. Inevitably there must be some conflict between these two sides of his nature. Indeed the exercise of our conscious reasoning ability has meant that we have lost to a large extent the desire or ability to view ourselves as animals, even though the solution to many social problems would become apparent if we did so.

A strong instinct which we have, at a very deep level, is for the survival of the species, modified at this stage of evolution to the survival of the race or tribe, which emerges consciously in most cases as nationalism or patriotism. Where the tribe and the nation do not coincide, trouble inevitably follows. Yet there seems no doubt that advanced or civilized (whatever that means) cultures or societies do not take this basic instinct into account in decisions taken about such things as national boundaries and other sources of trouble in their complex and possibly multi-racial social structures. We are conditioned to accept these structures from birth and in general only question them from a self-interested point of view. The self-interests of the individual or small group frequently conflict with the interests of the overall group, and we do not reason animalistically enough, an apparent contradiction in terms, when trying to resolve such social problems. For instance, it is no good attempting to force integration between tribal types. Therefore our social problems often remain unresolved. These conflicts occur much less often in animals or mammals having a much simpler social structure and smaller groupings, and are resolved according to their animal natures.

The next level of the survival instinct, after the survival of the species and the survival of the tribal group, but on a much more conscious plane and therefore of less significance to my argument, is the survival of the family group, and after that of the individual. All these instincts can be summed up as the survival of one's genes. All tend to have associated with them a territorial need.

Other forms of grouping, e.g. political or religious, can have an almost equally strong bonding power, but only because many people seem to need to believe in something or somebody, a need to be led.

It is clear from our world that man is still very much driven by his instincts in that his actions are mainly motivated by his simple animal needs, like food, sex, children and so on, which is to be expected. But there is a darker side. Ask a New York policeman if man is an animal. Or simply watch the act of sex. Or imagine social behaviour if the veneer of civilization were stripped away, and food and water became scarce. Only by making arrangements to accommodate this knowledge within our social structure will we improve it.

Desmond Morris in "The Naked Ape" states:-"Our civilizations will only be able to prosper if we design them such that they do not clash with our basic animal demands."

Chapter 2

Ethics and Evolution

Where does the line of reasoning in Chapter 1 lead us? Firstly to the supposition that what is fundamentally "good" could be defined as that which is supportive of the survival of the individual, family, tribe or species, in that order i.e. our most basic instincts. Evolution after all is based on survival itself being a fundamental driving instinct. This concept of "good" cannot therefore be just a moral, or ethical concept, it goes much deeper than that. When a man sacrifices himself to save others, the supreme example of a "good" act, he is overcoming the first level of the survival instinct by a supreme act of will, but is still acting in accordance with the more fundamental levels. Similarly assisting another person in their life, and thus in a sense their survival, is a "good" act. War is often the result of the tribal level of this survival instinct, and could sometimes therefore be seen as a "good" act from an individual point of view. Perhaps it can even contribute to the survival of the fittest. But if your brother happens to be fighting on the other side, well, you have a survival instinct problem in more ways than one. Indeed because you are actively assisting in preventing the survival of other persons, let alone your brother, you have a survival instinct problem anyway, often leading to psychological problems, most particularly when your enemy is of the same racial type as you. Incidentally we could view the motives behind the first political world war as being fairly stupid, whereas the second political world war was clearly "good" against "evil".

When our civilization is looked at from this fundamentally survivalist viewpoint of what is "good", many things become clearer. There are parallels in primate social structures where the basic laws at work can be clearly identified. For instance tribal rivalries, often in territorial defence, and sometimes (as with chimpanzees) leading to war, can be seen as instinctive reactions within species, including our own. Black / white conflict is clearly a tribal antipathy. Jewish persecution is a very good example. Dare I suggest that an enlightened approach to this very powerful instinct might be that controlled rather than random warfare could become an option for two small tribes or nations in dispute, all else having failed? At least until we manage to reach a more integrated and advanced stage of civilization.

Conversely the concept of "evil" could be seen as anything that works against the survival of an individual or individuals, and thus the survival and evolution of the species. From the latter viewpoint there is thus a natural antipathy towards the diseased and mentally aberrant. Taking it to one extreme, if the survival of a tribe is threatened, for instance by intermarriage with a tribe perceived as being physically or intellectually inferior, then the instinct would be to prevent that, and this should not be classed as an evil act. Intermarriage with an acceptable tribe might improve the gene variation and therefore be evolutionary desirable, but such an outcome could still clash with the tribal instinct. Practices such as homosexuality are clearly non-survivalist and therefore not in the general good, although most youths do pass through a brief homosexual phase during their teens, probably helping to bond with peers in the process of becoming a man.

Personal conscience with regard to how our acts affect others can be seen to be one result of the basic tribal or species survival instinct, since ideally it should guide our acts such that they are broadly "good" in the aiding of survival sense. Our lack of understanding of this (and also, incidentally, in the past, of the universe) has led to the rise of religion to act as personal conscience, thus neatly explaining and confirming for us the need for good acts. The belief that, in our personal life, everything is ultimately for the best is a commonly held belief, and very comforting, and implies that everything is pre-ordained anyway, which of course leads directly to a belief in God. Unfortunately religion has been in the past one of the greatest evils of our society. Its present development to a more tolerant and take-it-or-leave-it viewpoint, except for Islam, could possibly lead eventually to a single religion for the rest of mankind, at least for those who need it. Buddhism would be best, since it does not involve a God, but does advocate regard for your fellow man (and animals).

Mankind may eventually become entirely coffee-coloured, and evolve out the tribal instinct. It is our present tribal level instinct working against this, combined with the pace of modern technology having far out-stripped our ethical development, such as the development of nuclear weapons, genetic engineering and bio-technology, which poses a great short-term threat to mankind. Also of course over-population, since we try to prevent natural disasters, famine, disease and wars, which are natural check factors.

Effective action purely as a result of ethical reasoning is rare. Intelligence of course has only evolved as a favoured path for survival and evolution and has no "higher" meaning.

One can speculate that future evolution might be in the realms of overall mental rather than physical development. Modern medical care operates to some extent against the survival of the fittest, but really only as far as physical evolution is concerned. Mental evolution, for instance, as a very extreme example, in ESP ability (see later), and possibly via a mutation, might occur, provided it wasn't killed off as a new and threatening species. The phenomenon of autistic savants, whose brains function in a totally different way to ours, reveals the hidden potential within the depths of the human brain. A mutation could perhaps access this potential in the normal brain.

We could conceivably manipulate our own normal evolution by genetic engineering, a difficult task which we are nowhere near being able to handle ethically, and probably never will be. However, a natural mutation, or a genetically engineered one, if allowed to survive and multiply, could presumably in the far distant future be a mentally superior species, perhaps to some extent dependent for survival on advanced bio-technology, and would inevitably be competing with our species for survival on this planet. In imagination much the same is true of an alien species which might have contact with the earth in other than an altruistic frame of mind (such as in The Midwich Cuckoos, by John Wyndham).

Evolution does appear capable of allowing a broad range of development to exist at any given time, after all there are still present in the world Stone Age tribes, but probably only when such tribes are largely isolated, which is no longer the case. However there are many tribal groups, even in the civilized world, whose ethical and social development is backward, such as the Taliban. The process of evolution may or may not be random, but, as in quantum theory physics, it may well be uncertain. In "The Naked Ape", Desmond Morris has suggested that tribal cultural development in a competitive world forms part of the evolutionary process, which if you think about it could be viewed as a form of subtle racism, but has only a short-term effect on overall evolution.

We do not know how such things as behaviour and instincts are passed on, but we do know that the human gene pool is becoming flawed, in that evolution, i.e. natural selection, is becoming circumvented by modern social health measures. If indeed this is true, genetically propagated weaknesses, both physical and mental, will increase. Animal populations wax and wane in line with natural conditions by a process unknown to us, but the process must also apply to the human race, for instance the substantial increase in male births after a drastic war, or indeed new diseases appearing at a time when over-population is drastically affecting the environment (part of the Gaia concept mentioned in Chapter 8). Because of our interference in these processes the long-term scenario for our existence on earth is therefore perhaps suspect, despite, or more probably because of, our vast numbers, that is unless we begin to regulate our affairs, not only with regard to the survival of our environment, but also with regard to natural selection and to our animal nature, which is the burden of this chapter.

It is perhaps appropriate here to summarise the human condition. If one considers the early civilizations of Egypt and the Middle East, South America, China and Africa as beginning to appear, in general, roundabout 7000 years ago, then we have had some 7000 years of so-called civilization, yet we are still at each other's throats, usually for reasons of religion, race, politics or greed, or any combination of the four. Religions are a matter of blind faith in the myth of one religion over another, and the myth of a God or Gods, and lack common sense. Race implies very different mind-sets, and politics and greed are a matter of have and have-nots. How all these deep-seated opposites can be overcome in anything other than further thousands of years is difficult to see. One can only hope that eventually mankind can achieve some form of universal common sense, and concentrate on what, if we still exist by then, will probably be the survival of the species. Perhaps it is a threat to that survival which will be the catalyst.

Chapter 3

Environment

We should be seen as dependent on our environment, like any animal. The nature of man is inextricably tied to interaction with his own kind and to the earth from which he springs. Evolution involves adaptation to the environment. Our physical intake from nature such as air or food produces a transformation of energy which sustains us. Our susceptibility to the movement of heavenly bodies other than our own earth, mostly the sun and moon of course, is another example of our interaction with our environment. Changes in our environment are often cyclic or rhythmic, and sometimes involve positive feedback in a closed loop type of control action, which can produce long-term cataclysmic climate change, leading to times of rapid extinction, like the Ice Ages. Feedback both positive (wild fluctuations) and negative (gradually reducing the effect) gives rise to the idea of earth as a self-organising entity, which seems to characterise much in nature (part of the Gaia concept).

We perceive our environment by only five senses, although animals have others, such as a magnetic sense, and many aspects of the universe, like electro-magnetic radiations outside the narrow visible light part of the electro-magnetic spectrum, such as x-rays, are not directly detectable by us. There are other aspects of our universe which may not even be understandable by us, such as multi-dimensions, multi-universes, the origin of the Big Bang or even the true nature of energy. This is not surprising, since our intelligence is designed by evolution only to aid our survival and evolution, and the type of intelligence needed to achieve an understanding of the universe, if there is one, is not necessary for us to survive and evolve. But could it be achieved perhaps by an artificial intelligence (AI) which we might create? This view has some scientific backing, and is somewhat scary.

Almost any form of unregulated destruction of our environment is obviously pretty stupid, particularly when you remember that evolution is linked with adaptation to the environment.

Chapter 4

Character

If character is likened to a physical body, then genetic factors like one's basic brain cell pattern for one, amongst many others, create the skeleton of the body, as it were, and upbringing and environment factors can be seen as forming the flesh on the skeleton, including largely determining the neural connections and pathways linking the individual brain cells in the basic brain cell pattern. Another analogy would be hardware and software.

Intelligence seems to be spread across the whole brain, and it is considered that roughly half comes from inherited genes and half from upbringing and environment. Inherited characteristics perhaps determine the intellectual upper limit an individual can reach (basic brain cell pattern). Environment, upbringing, training and teaching (brain stimulation) up to about 3 ½ years old, perhaps determine how close eventually to the intellectual upper limit an individual can get, by maximising the early neural pathways of the brain (cf. identical twin studies). To give your child a good start in life, start teaching the 3 R's at age 2 ½, while the neural pathways are still forming. Intelligence improves with age up to a certain point, including the forging of some new neural pathways. It has also been shown that brain efficiency can be permanently improved by low-level electrical stimulation, which surely must be the first step towards a super-intelligent being – a boon or a disaster? Time will tell.

Our long-term memories appear for the most part to be unique to our species, and seem to be stored in various special parts of the brain, as in a computer – possibly in resonating neural networks. Our brains seem to have massively more potential than we use.

In this general context it is interesting to note the theory that gene modification can be achieved by learned behavioural factors, such as giraffe forebears stretching their necks for the higher leaves. Learning thus continues to modify inherited behavioural patterns present in genes, and even mental characteristics. The quotation from "The Naked Ape" mentioned towards the end of Chapter 2 supports this view. Incidentally there seems to be no organic need for sleep. It occurs perhaps only because man is a diurnal rather than a nocturnal animal, and vice versa for nocturnal animals.

Also incidentally it is interesting to note that the amount of sun over millennia may determine some of our tribal or racial characteristics e.g. colour or swarthiness, but also the more sun, the greater the volatility and possibly a mind-set with a greater susceptibility to brain-washing to some degree, although that is of course hugely controversial. For some such tribes or races life may be cheaper than for others, especially if they are fecund.

Chapter 5

Society

There is, in any animal group, a pecking order of precedence. Similarly there will always be a class structure in human society. Some will be leaders and some followers. Reasoned attempts to improve society can only succeed if they are, I reiterate, in accordance with the fundamental animal nature of man. This reasoning leads to obvious ways of improving society, such as recognising that much city violence is due to lack of personal "territory", as in experiments with over-crowded rats. Tower blocks were obvious recipes for disaster, despite having space between them. This is like having space around cages of over-crowded rats. Another aspect would be recognising the need for the young male to prove himself, particularly to his peers. This need can be seen to be catered for in any primitive human society…it even has a name – rite of passage, but has been lost sight of in modern society, which places too much emphasis on the moral approach. Our society attempts to control human animalistic behaviour with a moral code of conduct backed by the law, but to derive these morals or laws from anything other than the animal behaviour viewpoint, for instance to derive them from a religious viewpoint, is to err. In our modern society every young man who chooses should, at the age of sixteen, be sent off to his proving test, which can take many forms, even simply passing exams and university, but otherwise should involve some danger and the endurance of pain. The outcome is a sense of self-respect and the respect of his peers. In a society without this rite of passage, and where young men can see no effective future, they will resort to a gang culture and criminality in order to fulfil this instinct of proving themselves to their peers. Similarly, surely it's possible for unemployed people and even prisoners to be given sensible work to do by a government agency. Also state-controlled brothels should be possible, without any demeaning of the women involved, and there may always be women who would be prepared to earn a living in this way. These would be major steps forward in our society, since they would result in a massive decrease in criminality, as would government takeover of illegal drug dealing, with the aim of reducing addiction rather than increasing it.

On another tack, and with more chance of actually happening, the discovery of the human genome together with the pressures of over-population will, at some future time, bring in genetic screening of foetuses. The discovery that mental abnormalities including homosexuality are very probably based on defective genes, and also physical abnormalities such as tendency to cancer, clearly introduces the idea that such gene-based variations or mutations, possibly in the latter case caused by environmental pollution, could be corrected by gene manipulation. They are variations which are non-beneficial and which, but for our social and medical ethics, would eventually vanish naturally through the survival of the fittest. So the genetic engineering of foetuses will bring gene therapy or gene manipulation (and abortion) options, at first voluntary. Soon, however, under the pressure of increasing population, diminishing resources and social and medical expenditure problems, mandatory action will have to exist. Then, within perhaps a generation, many of mankind's social problems could be solved. The problems will of course be firstly who will decide, and secondly what range of variation in the genes will be acceptable. What about genes giving susceptibility to criminal or aberrant behaviour? What about mutated genes? Was eugenics right in principle? But, if solved, what a potential breakthrough for the human race. We will effectively have adopted one of the great principles of nature, the survival of the fittest, at last. Given good education for all, Utopia may loom. Or complete disaster.

Studies indicate that the best size of social group appears to be around one hundred. Thus modern city life causes severe tensions from this viewpoint also. From the animalistic viewpoint a male group, for instance a workers union, would have the same instincts as a hunting group, in that it works for the common good of the group. A young male group, or gang, would aim at usurping adult male positions in the tribal group, especially if the tribal group is too large for a self-controlling factor to exist.

There will be, in a society, those individuals who cannot integrate, or are otherwise undesirable, as in the case of recidivist criminals, or some parasitic traveller groups. What does the animal society do in such cases? Such individuals are sometimes killed but more often permanently isolated from the group, and either exist like that or die quickly, and do not reproduce. We have our prisons and institutions for isolation, but we do not recognise the evolutionary desirability of not allowing recidivist individuals to return to the group, or even perhaps to reproduce. This is, most would say, a victory for our "higher" moral viewpoint, but in fact such individuals are actively negative as far as "good" acts (according to the previous definition) are concerned. If society can afford it, as ours can, then measures to correct the aberrant behaviour are reasonable, in the hope that the individual will become a positive rather than a negative member of society. An animal group is prevented from breeding from such suspect stock by the automatic control mechanism found in such groups, such as the isolationism already mentioned. We should follow the same instincts. If we had always done so, this statement would not arouse controversy. We have lost such instinctive behaviour. Truly amoral persons, not only choosing to live not according to the rules of society, but continually committing acts which attempt to break down that society, for whatever motive, should thus be removed from that society. However there is the dilemma, as with anyone who transgresses the rules of a complex society, of who decides between correction attempts (which should be what prisons and borstals do), permanent isolation (if ever possible) or removal (painless capital punishment). Punishment is only of use in the deterring of others, and is not much good even at that, except perhaps in the case of capital punishment. In the case of violent crime how pleasant it would be if justice and the human rights of the victim could be served by allowing the victim to choose that whatever was done to him or her should be done to the perpetrator. It seems only fair after all. An eye for an eye. Some males seem to seek violence. I suppose the army is the place for them. Our jury system of peers is good except they are only peers in the sense that they are human beings, and are liable to have all sorts of prejudices and all sorts of intelligences. Perhaps it would be better to rely on experience and have a jury of elders, as in primitive societies.

There is the principle involved here of "does the end justify the means?" The ultimate ends are, as with instincts, first of all the health and survival of self, then the family, then the tribe and finally the health and survival and continued evolution of the species, mankind. Genetic health and survival in effect. Or perhaps, "the greatest good for the greatest number". In general the justifiable means, similar to the definition of what is "good", is any act which supports, or does not act negatively upon, the end aim of being a positively acting member of society, including helping to correct, isolate or eliminate aberrances or aberrants. Political views lead to different interpretations here, and indeed during different stages in the evolution of a society very different political structures may succeed one another and may be best at the time, like communism, but leading to very different approaches to social problems.

When considering the precepts above there is, of course, often a fine moral or ethical line to be drawn. We must remember the Nazi excuse of obeying orders, and in their case the end was not a desirable one. But things are not always black and white. Society and particularly governments don't have a conscience, only man does. Our adversarial approach to democratic politics (the party system), and to the pursuit of justice (the prosecutor / defender system) sometimes seems to lack common sense. The advantage of the democratic political system is that it provides checks and balances on government, but perhaps the future will find a better system of democracy, and also of justice. For instance some system of consensus, and in the case of justice, the discovery of the truth by allowing the use of harmless drugs on suspects, or the use of an efficient form of lie detector. Also the Scottish verdict of "Not Proven" should surely be a universal possibility, leaving open the chance for further investigation, or awaiting improvement in forensic methods. At least we have got rid of the ridiculous Double Jeopardy law. Also a jury of elders rather than peers, as mentioned above, and allowing the jury to ask questions of the defence and prosecution before retiring. And surely common sense dictates that criminals should not be able to get away with crimes because of technicalities. At the moment in deciding on prosecution there are two main problems. The problem of a suspect refusing to respond to police questioning is partly addressed by the Miranda ritual, which should include a definite statement to the effect that failure to answer questions may be interpreted by the court as an indication of guilt. The problem of witness intimidation is more difficult and is only partly addressed by an upgraded re-location i.e. a bribe by the state. Only worth it in big cases. At the moment in several ways the law is weighted in favour of the criminal.

When considering conflicts between groups, both sides could be justified since, at the present stage of evolution, the end is the health, survival and evolution of the group or tribe, rather than mankind. The tribal base of this instinct is still clearly very strong in our world, since every man knows that all-out war may be suicidal for mankind, yet still the tribal instinct is stronger than the species instinct. It may require the future dominance of multi-national conglomerates to overcome tribal barriers to global integration, or it may take a threat to the world as a whole from somewhere, either natural or alien, to unite mankind as a single group. If this lasted long enough, with of course the united group intermarrying among itself, then the survival and evolution instinct would become directed towards mankind as a species, and this would be happening because, in the case of aliens, man would have realised that his intelligence and ability to survive and evolve was not unique, and that he may be competing for survival.

Laws are the rules that enable a complex society to exist. If they are based on the animalistic approach, they will be positive in effect. However, even when imperfect, there can be no justification for breaking them in a democracy, even in an attempt to correct unjust laws. That way lies anarchy, which is massively negative in effect. It is useful to remember, when considering why social structures succeed or fail, that mankind is essentially selfish, as we have said, which is simply accepting the basic animal premise of looking after oneself and one's family. A structure which recognises this is likely to prosper. It's probably the main reason why communism eventually fails, because it is fundamentally flawed in this way, together with the fact that man is essentially competitive (and capitalist) by nature.

A pecking order is always present in a social group, which tells us that all men are not equal, and never can be. They may be created equal, but that's as far as it goes. Some will turn out to be leaders, and some will be followers and some will be neither. Similarly any society should realise that a competitive instinct exists in the human psyche, as well as the other instincts. A capitalist society would seem to cater for this, despite the divisiveness it also engenders. Unfortunately capitalism has no discernable ethics, or you could say that profit has no conscience. Governments should, I emphasise should, have that. Ethics and big business are like oil and water, they do not mix. Self-regulation of virtually any organisation is a myth. Self-interest isn't. No need to quote examples of this, recent history is enough.

Capitalism (i.e. profit) now funds most research. This has to be bad. Research should be controlled by far-thinkers. On a similar tack and put simplistically and harshly politics could be said to be based on pragmatism and expediency, sometimes stated as "will it work and can I get away with it?" Politics isn't entirely like that of course, but I don't think anyone would suggest that modern-day democracy is a perfect system. It has very little to do with a positive approach to what is "good" as previously defined, which should be the basis of all such thinking and decisions, although I suppose that is expecting a bit too much. Similarly in many of the world's institutions and governments the main reason for seeking office is as an opportunity for corruption. (Indeed the American voting system, especially for President, encourages corruption). And if not for corruption it is for personal aggrandisement. In very few cases is it out of an altruistic desire to serve the community.

The family unit is obviously positive and the feedback action is that if the family conforms to the rules it can prosper. However in our tower blocks one can come across examples of badly dysfunctional families, such as the obese, pasty-faced, low IQ, fecund single mother living off the state and resulting from several generations of poverty, bad environment and education and probably increasingly defective genes. The children have little chance. They grow up in the same way, proliferate and generally have a negative effect on society whilst being a drain on its resources. Their contribution is to increasingly debase the gene pool, yet society supports them and preserves their lives. Nature attempts some regulation in that their life span is generally shorter, partly due to their life style. It's the survival of the fittest attempting to work. But a society is defective where such families have come to exist, are maintained, and continue to exist. As has been said, drastic forms of education must be the answer.

Of course the ability to live longer due to modern health care is a good thing, providing one's working life is similarly extended, because of the greater experience that can be brought to bear in one's life and for the benefit of society. However it doesn't help the over-population problem.

Any democratic society should operate a national identity card system, together with a DNA database. Law abiding citizens would have nothing to fear.

The gregarious instinct to go with the crowd is very strong, and this can be perverted to evil ends quite easily, often by oratory, simply because it is so strong, especially when the tribal or other basic instincts are invoked. In local form, i.e. crowds, this is an example of the "Group Life Field" mentioned in Chapter 8 at work, but in an intensive mode rather than the background mode discussed in that chapter.

Human nature often produces acts which work against the good of the greater number, for instance when individuals accumulate wealth. A kibbutz or clan approach to society involving small social groups might be perceived as better, and also provides better opportunity for control of the animal side of human nature. Personal development in this environment is better as there are fewer false values to be chased. Everyone receives a good basic education and in essence it is the ideal form of communism, since it is also democratic. However such an approach, with race, class, religion, union membership and the like being totally without relevance, would probably still lead to inter-kibbutz rivalries just like inter-tribal rivalries. It's the competitive instinct. And individuals would still seek to advance themselves.

In our society we see the poor results achieved by trying to force integration between disparate groupings, which only succeeds in increasing prejudice on both sides. If true integration can ever be achieved in such a disparate society as ours, or indeed the world's, and in the absence of aliens or a great natural disaster, it can only come by leaving well alone over many generations, with intermarriage, but even then not without bloodshed at some times, one suspects.

All emotions are expressions of an underlying instinct. Love in particular is simply an intense instinct needed to ensure bonding and frequent insemination with a desirable member of the opposite sex, i.e. one probably having good genes. The basis of love is sexual attraction. The beauty of it is that reproduction by sexual means not only serves our instinct for the survival of our own individual genes, but also provides the diversification necessary for evolution, evolution being increasingly better adaptation to an evolving environment, not just a mechanism for the intrinsic improvement of the species. Aging and death are necessary for evolution to occur, so extending life spans wouldn't help from that point of view. Sorry if you were banking on it.

I propose the creation of a new political party, the Humanity Party, whose aim would be to promote the principles outlined in this book, but very gradually. There might well come a time when such a move might be welcomed.

Chapter 6

Free Will

The animalistic view of man and society has some interesting implications. It means that given complete knowledge of character and circumstances, actions should be predictable i.e. there would be no free will, but in practice the equation is complex enough to mean that effectively a free choice is made. However it is true to say that given reasonable knowledge of character or personality, of which there are certain fundamental types (and evolution, in the interests of the common good, has led to the development of associated facial types or characteristics), the future of an individual may be broadly predicted, although with much uncertainty of course. A factor that seems to support this is the evidence gained from twins separated at birth, who often seem to live extraordinarily similar lives. There seems to be a certain justice in life within a society, which is broadly that as you sow, so shall you reap. Genes may help to pre-determine even what seem to be random events in a life. New research shows that unconscious processes precede any conscious decisions, and that therefore, together with the considerations above, perhaps free will is an illusion, as it is in the animalistic view of mankind.

Chapter 7

Gender

The role of women seen from the animalistic point of view is domestic. Modern society is producing alternative options, leading to some stress. One could say that in general a woman is not fulfilling her animal instincts if she does not at some time mate and produce a family. The same is true of a man, and he has the role of provider. These are basic animal instincts and a society which disregards them, as with all such instincts, does so at its peril. It is probable that women would make a much better job of running the world, but I think it's true to say that they don't, in general, seem to want to.

In a relationship in general it is the basic instincts that predominate. Man, provider, woman, homemaker. A man must earn and retain the respect of a woman, and he must continually re-affirm his love for her. These are the two things she needs from him. A woman must keep the man sexually contented, and be a good mother. These are the two things he needs from her. Obvious generalities they may be, but nonetheless true, and often forgotten.

Chapter 8

The Group Life Field
(or Group Mind Interaction)

I would like to postulate the existence of what could be called the Group Life Field (GLF). Physically it would be compounded of the faint electro-magnetic emanations arising from the electrical activity along the neurological pathways of the brain, or mind. Each individual in a group would both contribute to, and be affected by, the GLF. The simultaneous changes of direction observed in large flocks of birds or shoals of fish would be examples of the GLF at work. Or the fact that in many groups of mammals if one individual learns a desired behaviour trait, all seem to know, and thus accelerate evolution. In an emotional crowd individuality may temporarily vanish almost completely, and this can be very frightening. If the GLF exists it ought to be "good" in the survival and evolutionary sense, and therefore may be expected eventually to evolve more fully than at present in gregarious species, such as man. It is instinctive in modern man to belong to a group or groups i.e. to be gregarious, perhaps because of the influence of the GLF.

A physical explanation of how the GLF manifests itself in flocks or shoals or colonies of large numbers is found in computer simulations of, for instance, the behaviour of swirling convocations of starlings. It appears that only 3 rules need to be obeyed by any individual in the group in order to simulate this behaviour. Firstly all individuals must fly at the same speed. Secondly each individual must do the same as the nearest six or possibly seven individuals, and that would be impossible for a single individual to keep track of without the GLF, and thirdly, and of less importance to our GLF thesis, that avoiding action is taken when a predator appears. Interestingly the same idea can be applied to the movement of human crowds, in that the average walking speed is 1.3 m/s, we tend to move in straight lines and form lanes, and we take avoiding action.

This GLF concept could be why "good" has a spiritual connotation. The GLF would be an aspect of nature, so in a sense earth's Nature, with all its complexities, can be seen as our "God".

The mind can be extremely powerful in controlling the body, as seen in the placebo effect, or in yoga control of body functions normally beyond the control of the conscious mind. Also the lower levels of our minds seem to have associated with them ancestral memories and instincts which can determine actions. These ideas may tie in with the GLF concept.

The brain is in a delicate chemical, electrical and biological balance which is easily upset e.g. by magnetic or electric fields, or chemical or botanical drugs, possibly leading to "paranormal" experiences often of a similar nature e.g. Near Death Experiences, LSD effects, and even ghostly phenomena in the case of fields. These are physically normal rather than paranormal since they are neurologically based.

For most people, when moving around in pitch darkness, there is a sense of proximity to a large object. This can only be due to the presence of a static field of some sort around the body – an aura. The presence of such a static field supports the idea of the GLF, and also the possible phenomenon of ESP.

Malevolent energy such as the possible poltergeist phenomenon could be a negative form of GLF. And If a person becomes fundamentally evil i.e. continually commits acts against the survival and evolution of one or more people, for whatever motive, then their interaction with the GLF would be to detract from it. The ultimate state to which man may strive in some eastern religions by mental development and training, Nirvana, or Prana, could be a form of communication with the GLF. Evolution may go this way, since it must be a favoured evolutionary path. On death some independent form of energy may be released to join the GLF, and may even linger locally in some way as an apparently supernatural or paranormal phenomenon, another explanation of ghosts, in a sort of local reversal of the law of entropy, tapping local natural energy, like magnetism, triggered by and perceptible only by an organism, and perhaps looping through time in some way.

The transmigration of souls is a concept which fits these general ideas, as is the idea of a Holy Spirit.

Poltergeist phenomena or the ability of dowsers possibly underline the existence of unknown biologically interacting fields. Is it possible to do proper scientific research on these things? It seems to be all too hazy for serious scientists to consider. Indeed the presence of consciousness, or of an observer, may play a part in something like poltergeist phenomena, as it does in quantum mechanics.

The concept of mind, although based on energy interaction in the brain, seems to be on a higher plane than just energy interaction, much as the possible mechanism of ESP or psychokinesis (PK) is perhaps on a higher plane than simple electro-magnetic radiation. We, of course, are limited to our five senses, and even they are limited in scope, for instance our eyes only react to a very small (light) part of the overall electro-magnetic spectrum. Thus other aspects of physical phenomena may be closed to us, as is, for instance, x-ray electro-magnetic radiation. The GLF is on a higher (or deeper) plane still and beyond our five senses. If it were not, we could tamper with it, which would not be, at our stage of evolution, evolutionary desirable.

The GLF may influence the evolution of a species. Also evolution may favour the development of the GLF via a feedback effect, as may have occurred in the past, but possibly when the evolutionary time was not right, and so the line or mutation died out. Neanderthal man (and possibly aboriginals) may be or have been examples of this, which would support the possibility of Neanderthal man having been perceived by Cro-Magnon man as a superior species, and therefore a threat and therefore to be wiped out.

It is possible that birth rate and the population of boys / girls born at any time, e.g. after wars, may be self-regulatory in some way beneficial to survival and evolution, and this may be an effect of the GLF (also see the Gaia concept below).

Man deprived of contact with the environment of earth and thus with the GLF would be under some stress, and this is evident in the so-called Astronaut Syndrome. Human biology interacts strongly with the earth environment (see Supernature by Lyall

Watson) as is evident in our biorhythms. Incidentally it is interesting that mathematics is the basis of physics but also of organic life. Examples of the latter are natural logarithm-based shell structures, theories of cyclic variation, the catastrophe theory of sudden organic events, like the sudden opening of a flower, and chaos fractal theory.

The Gaia theory of James Lovell is that all life, particularly bacteria and life at that level (on which all other life is based), interacts with the environment and gives rise to a self-regulation of nature by feedback between nature and entropy to maintain constant conditions. Sounds complicated but it's really a simple concept. An instance is the constant oxygen content of the air, despite the fact that such constancy is most unusual in our planetary conditions. We of course are close to destroying many natural checks and balances. Man's destructive influence on Gaia may lead to a catastrophic event i.e. a point where the Gaia balance collapses very suddenly.

There is a major perturbation every seventy four million years due probably to returning comet showers (the Nemesis concept) and a new biosphere life cycle arises after each cataclysm, and also to a lesser extent after natural global extinctions, of which there have been several, such as the asteroid impact which wiped out the dinosaurs. Perhaps future mankind will be able to arrange its own survival, passing through these cataclysms and ensuring the continuation of its GLF. Let us believe it will be so, and that by then man has a wisdom worth preserving. Your life and my life are but tiny steps on the way.

I present here an article by David Nicholson-Lord:-

"The good ship Scientific Orthodoxy is riding a little lower in the water today. Whatever Newton and Descartes said, it appears that Nature may yet have a mind of its own.

An experiment involving 103 Nottingham students and four crossword puzzles from the London Evening Standard is claimed to have provided "partial" support for the theory that living things have a form of collective biological memory, able to communicate across barriers of time and space.

The theory of morphic resonance, the brainchild of Rupert Sheldrake, the Cambridge biologist, created a furore when it was first advanced in 1981.

Nature described Dr. Sheldrake's book, A New Science of Life, as "fit for burning" and mainstream scientists condemned it as a retreat into mysticism and magic. But the book became a best-seller and the ideas have achieved wide currency and something of a cult status.

His hypothesis of formative causation seeks to explain why people learn Morse code more quickly than a similar but bogus version, what decides the crystalline form of new substances and why it is that after one generation of rats has learnt a trick, succeeding generations, in different places appear to learn the same trick more quickly.

It is also claimed to offer clues to the spread of blue tits' expertise with milk bottle tops and to the observed rise in the average score in IQ tests as more people have taken them. The theory suggests that non-material "morphogenetic (form-shaping) fields" exist, able to transcend conventional physical barriers and working "as if nature has a memory for the shapes of things". Critics regard it as an up-dated version of the "world-mind" of ancient science and eastern philosophy.

The California-based Institute of Noetic Sciences has announced that three students, two of them British, have been awarded a $5000 (£3000) prize in a world-wide competition for an experiment to test the theory. The three entries tended to confirm it, although this was not a condition of entry. The judges, all senior academics, included Professor Patrick Bateson, provost of King's College, Cambridge. Experiments were judged for their "scientific elegance"

In Nottingham, students were given four crossword puzzles, two of which were unpublished when the experiment began. Those who attempted the "Easy Puzzle" after it had been published did better than those who tried it before it was published.

Another experiment at Oxford involved flashing strings of letters – some of them words, some nonsense – on a computer screen. It found that actions repeated by one group of people were easier for others to learn. In the third prize-winning entry, an Australian schoolboy demonstrated that there may be a morphic field associated with a language which makes it easier to remember.

Dr. Sheldrake said the entries were of a "very high calibre" and hoped they would lead to further research on the theory. John Maddox, editor of Nature, questioned the value of the tests and said they left the theory "in the dirt, where it has always been" ".

I further present part of an article by William Rees-Mogg (Richard Dawkins' ideas of the evolution of complex structures by multiple small steps came later):- .

"The French philosopher Henri Bergson suggested there was a general force which, as it were, applied intelligence to evolution. If one adopts these ideas of an intelligent force outside ourselves, a number of difficult problems are resolved. The first is the apparently universal human instinct for religion. If there were such a universal consciousness, it would be likely to be recognised as sacred. The place of the Holy Spirit in Christianity is of this character, as is the idea of the logos in Plato or in St. John's Gospel.

Another problem that would be resolved is the nature of certain types of mental illness. Schizophrenia often produces hallucinations of an external bombardment by spiritual forces, sometimes interpreted as radio rays. Schizophrenics can have visions of the divine. Whatever the current diagnosis of his illness, Christopher Smart, the eighteenth century poet, appears to have been suffering from a breakdown of mental limits on the inflow of divine consciousness. Dostoevsky describes similar passages in an epileptic condition. And terrible panics can also be seen by the mentally ill as invasions from outside.

This transmission theory also removes the difficulty of admitting, cautiously, the reality of some psychic phenomena. It is hard to exclude all the evidence for telepathy, precognition, inspired conversions, clairvoyance, out–of-body or near death experiences, or even for levitation or ghosts. There is too much evidence, from people of good reputation, for an absolute a priori refusal to accept any of it to be rational.

The chief scientific difficulty of neo-Darwinism itself, that random genetic change could not account for the sequence of development of some complex structures, was criticised by Bergman 80 years ago, and is now being explored in the laboratory. If there were a universal source of consciousness, transmitted through the brain, as oxygen is through the lungs, its influence might explain what appears to be the purposive development of complex structures that require multiple mutations to be effective.

William James, in his doctrine of pragmatism, used results as a test of truth. The transmission theory of the brain has the advantage that it solves problems, rather than creating them. The problem of the human instinct for religion, the problem of the inrushes experienced in some mental illnesses, the problem of psychic phenomena and the problem of pure randomness in neo-Darwinism are real difficulties for the scientific world view.

The Schiller-James-Bergson theory proposes a natural force of intelligence, which is perhaps received and transmitted by the brain, and also influences evolution in the direction of survival. That would restore purpose to nature, but it would also make possible the concept of human survival after death. Such a theory is repugnant to many scientists, but it is not contradicted by scientific observation.

Indeed, it can contain scientific facts that are difficult to fit with the pure randomness required by orthodox neo-Darwinism. If this theory were to be accepted, it would reconcile the division of human thought that has done so much harm in the past century and a half."

And that is the end of this rather rambling treatise on the Possible Future of Society. Although you may disagree with much of it, I hope it has at least provided food for thought, and more importantly has been worth the time you spent on it.